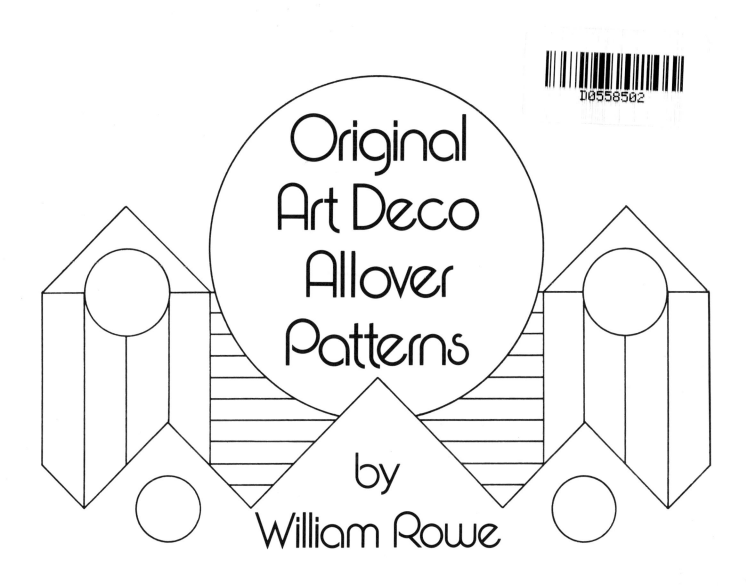

Original Art Deco Allover Patterns

by

William Rowe

DOVER PUBLICATIONS, INC., New York

Publisher's Note

William Rowe has developed a striking and original approach to creating patterns in the Art Deco style. On pages 2–45, he presents a basic repeat unit for an allover pattern on the left-hand page and, on the facing right-hand page, examples of how the unit can be adapted. All the material—the unit and its adaptations—is immediately usable as finished art in its own right, while also serving as a source of inspiration and a lesson in the use of black and white.

Copyright © 1989 by Dover Publications, Inc.
All rights reserved under Pan American and International Copyright Conventions.

Published in Canada by General Publishing Company, Ltd., 30 Lesmill Road, Don Mills, Toronto, Ontario.

Original Art Deco Allover Patterns is a new work, first published by Dover Publications, Inc., in 1989.

DOVER *Pictorial Archive* SERIES

This book belongs to the Dover Pictorial Archive Series. You may use the designs and illustrations for graphics and crafts applications, free and without special permission, provided that you include no more than ten in the same publication or project. (For permission for additional use, please write to Dover Publications, Inc., 31 East 2nd Street, Mineola, N.Y. 11501.)

However, republication or reproduction of any illustration by any other graphic service whether it be in a book or in any other design resource is strictly prohibited.

Manufactured in the United States of America
Dover Publications, Inc., 31 East 2nd Street, Mineola, N.Y. 11501

Library of Congress Cataloging-in-Publication Data

Rowe, William, 1946–
    Original art deco allover patterns / by William Rowe.
        p.   cm. — (Dover pictorial archive series) (Dover design library)
    ISBN 0-486-26139-5
        1. Decoration and ornament—Art deco.   2. Repetitive patterns (Decorative arts)
    I. Title.   II. Series.   III. Series: Dover design library.
NK1396.A76R69   1989
745.4'492—dc20   89-11936
                                                                          CIP

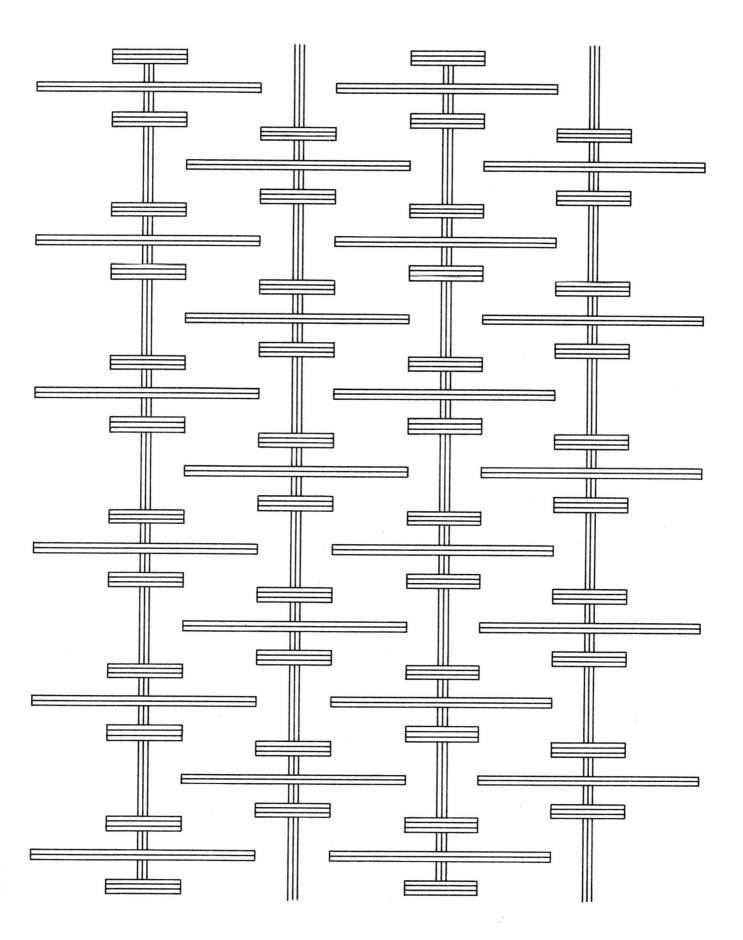

1

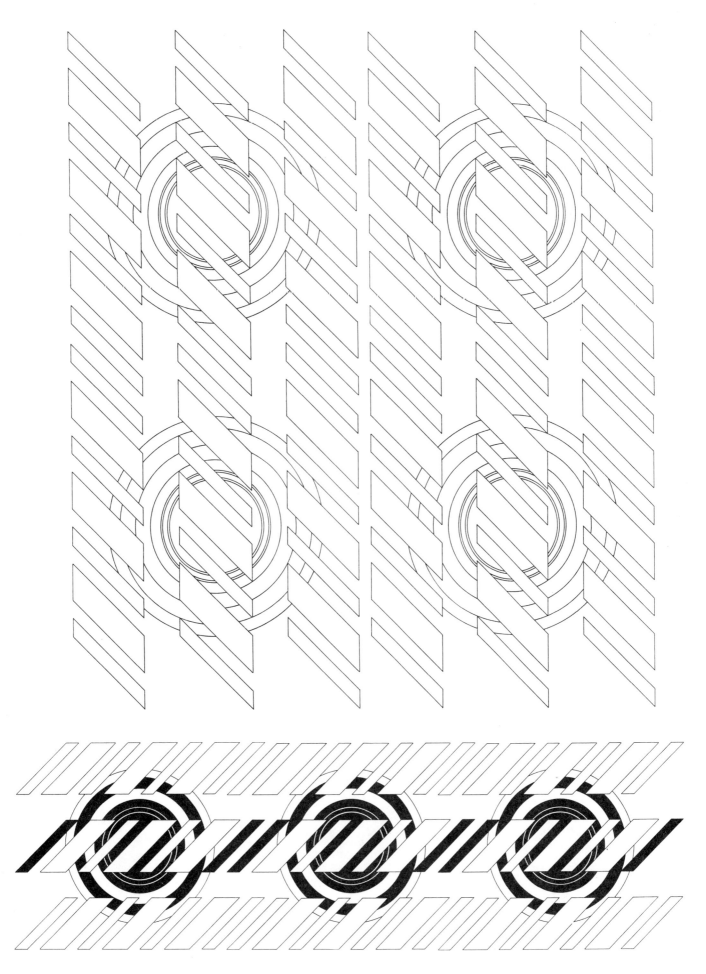

5

6

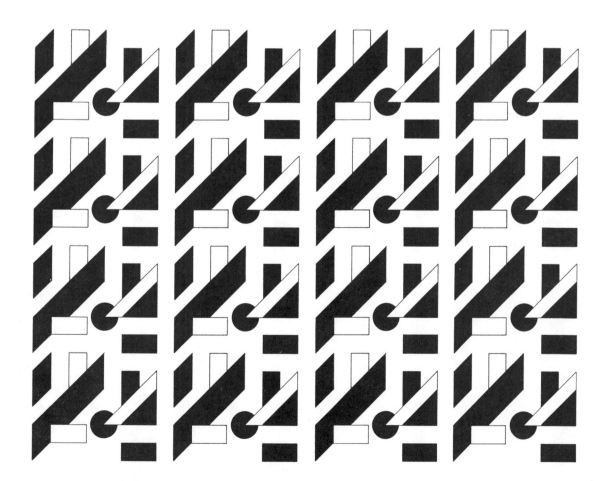

8

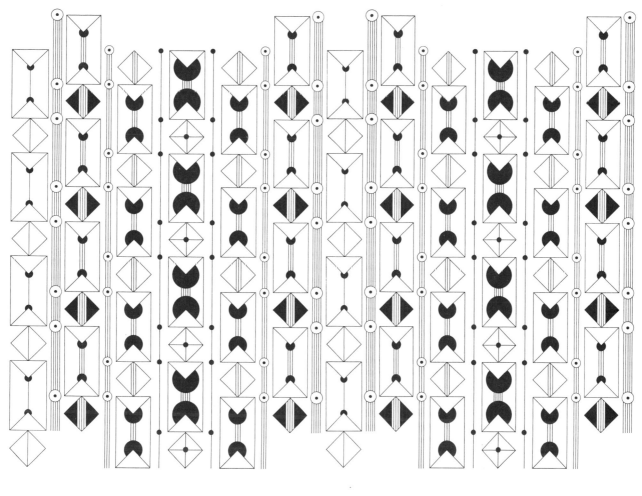

9

10

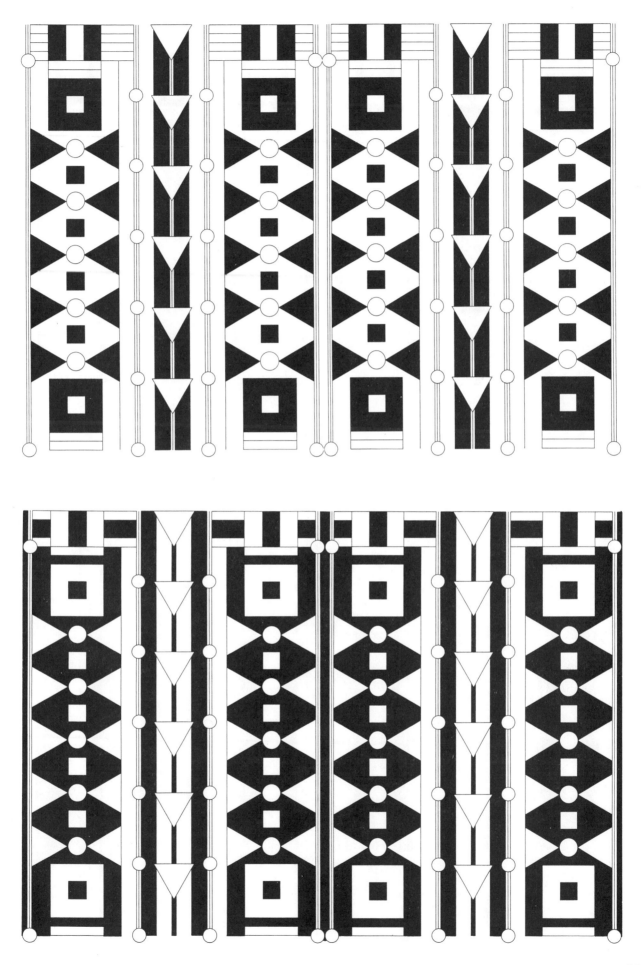

11

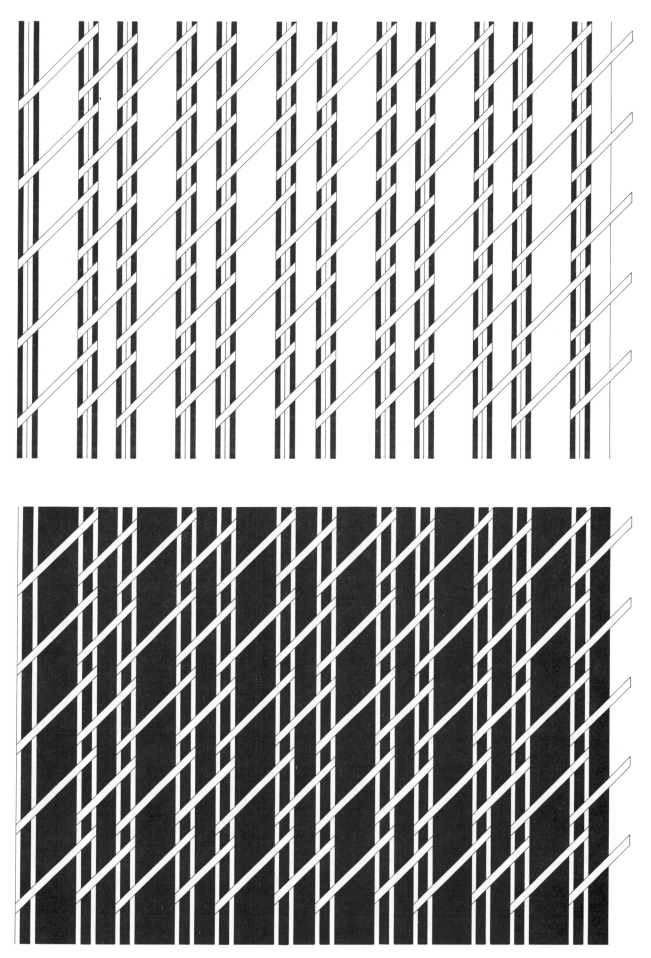

13

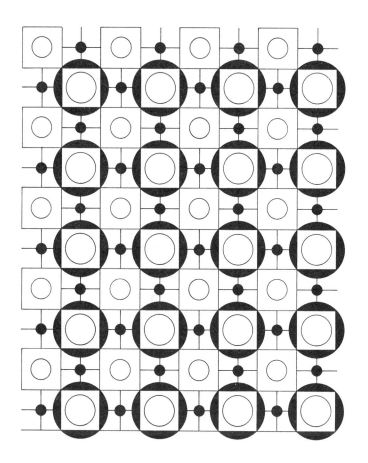

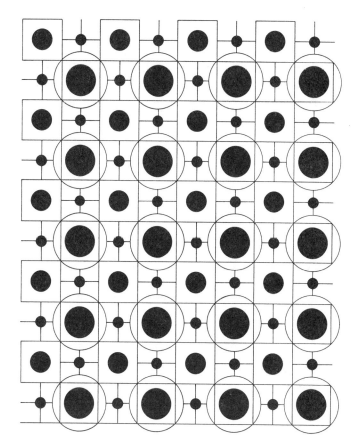

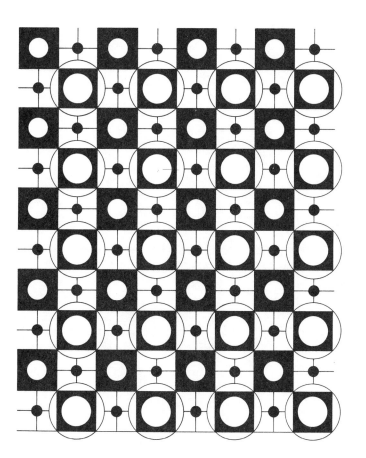

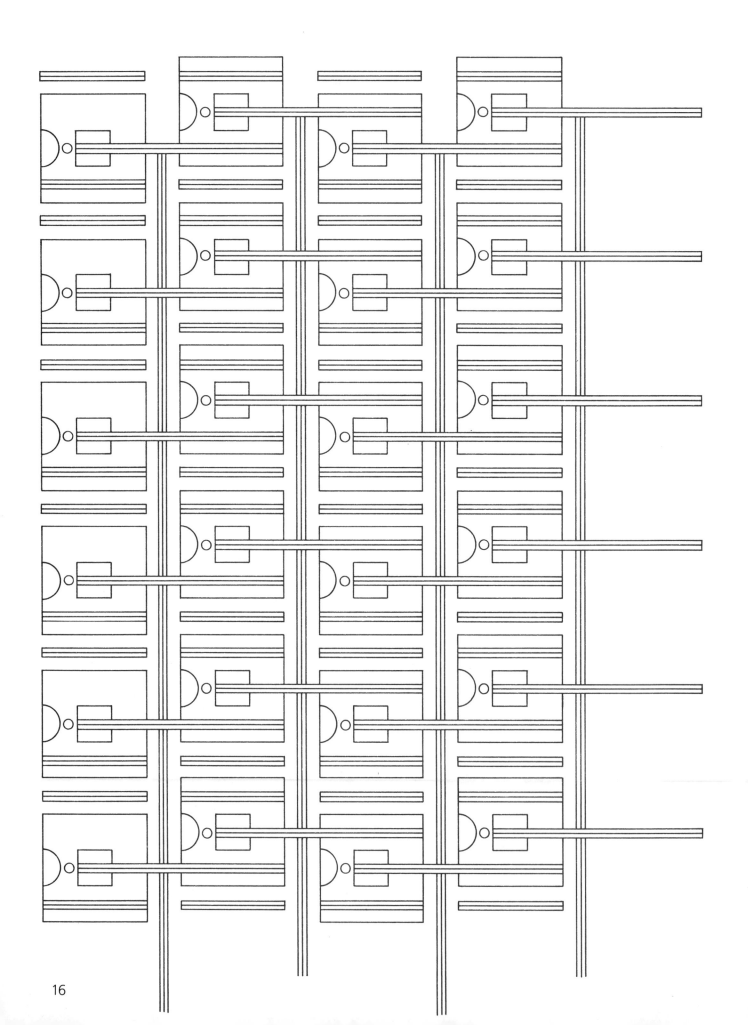

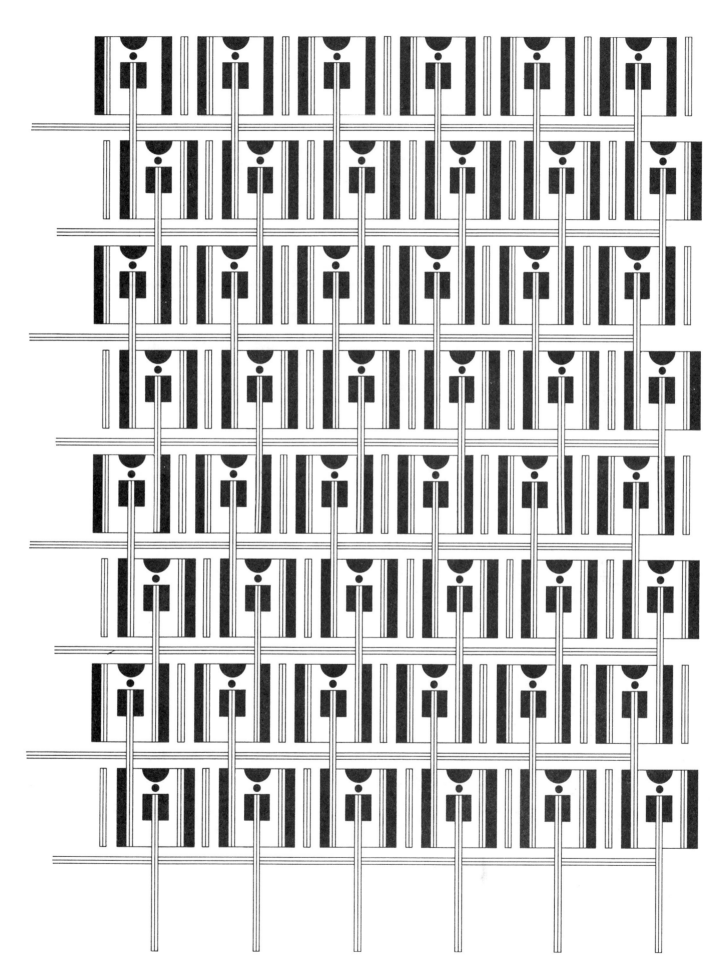

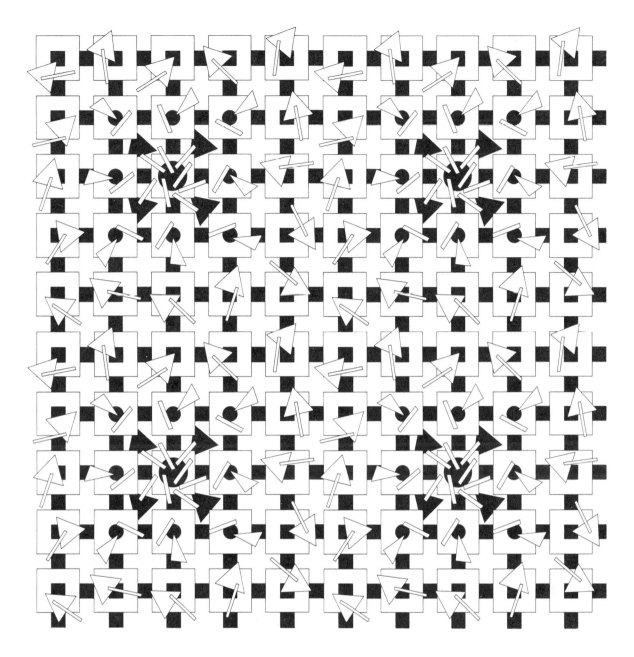

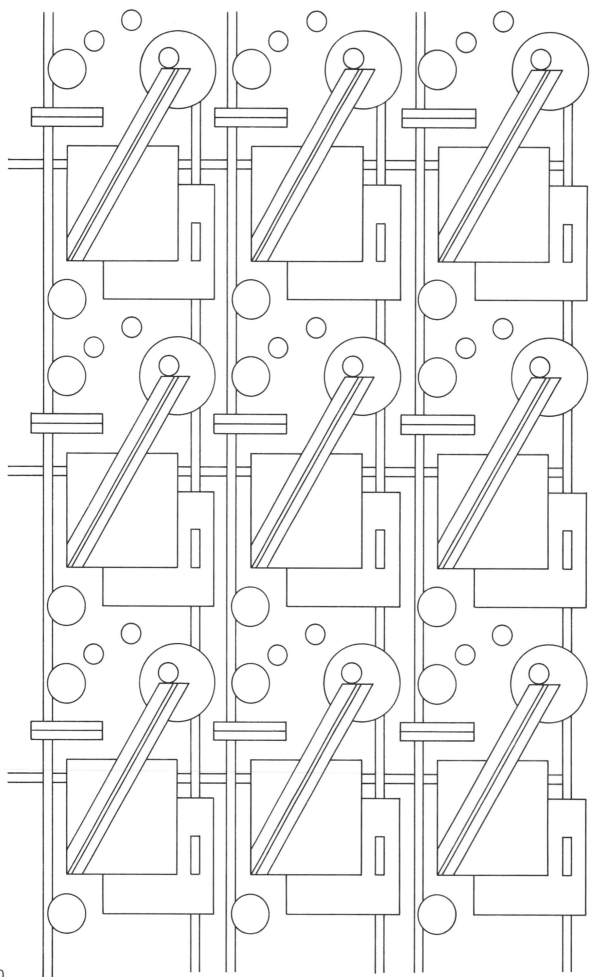

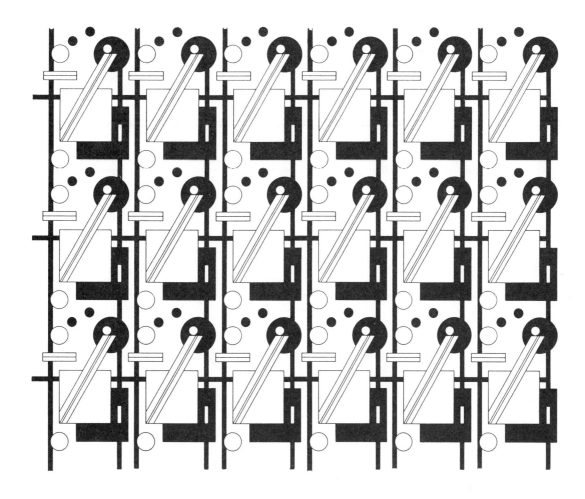

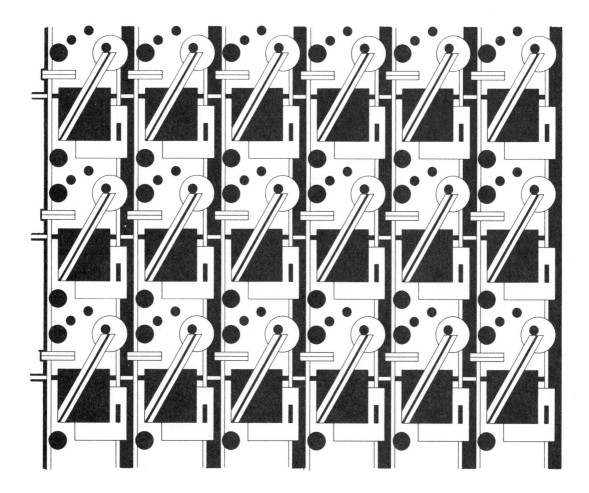

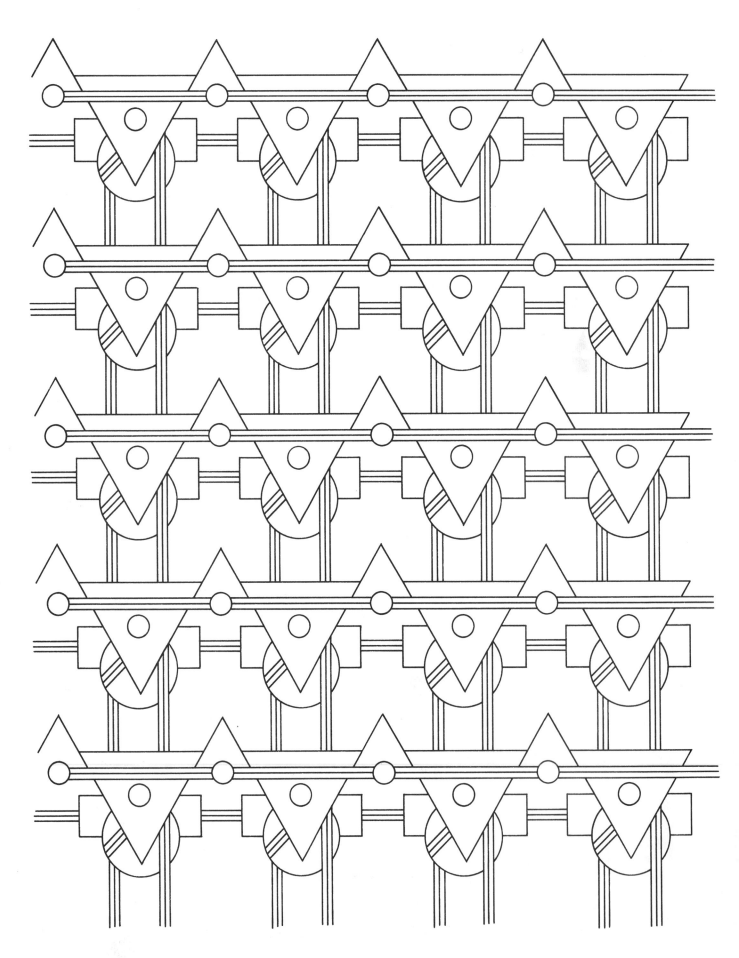

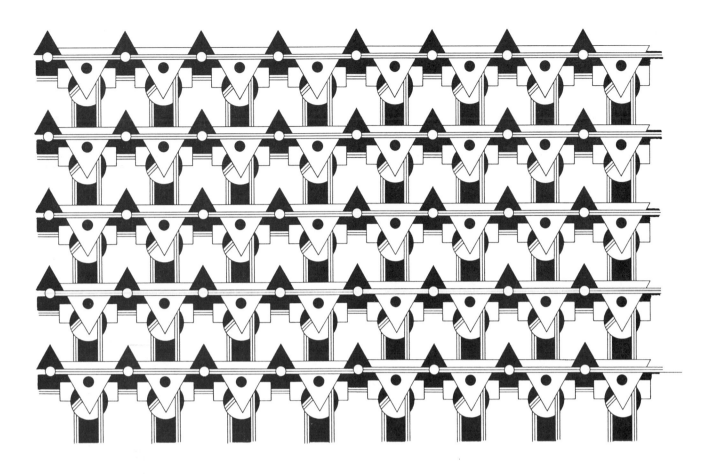

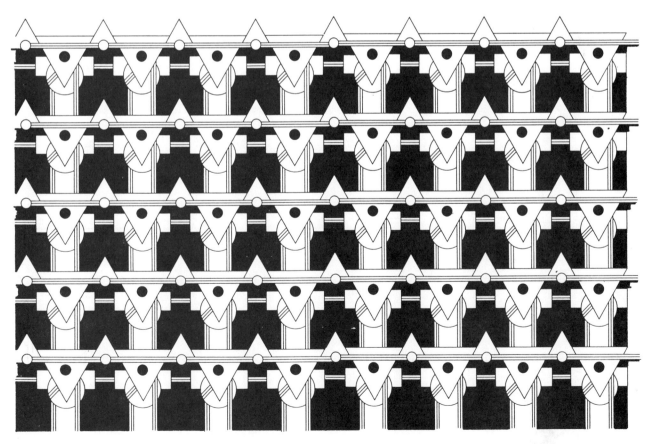

25

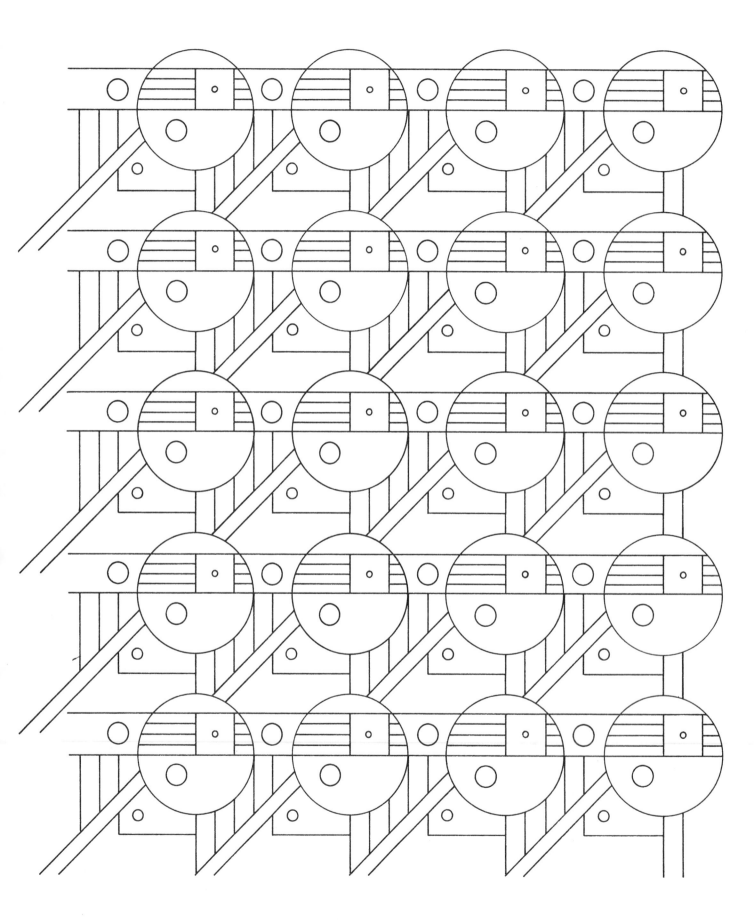

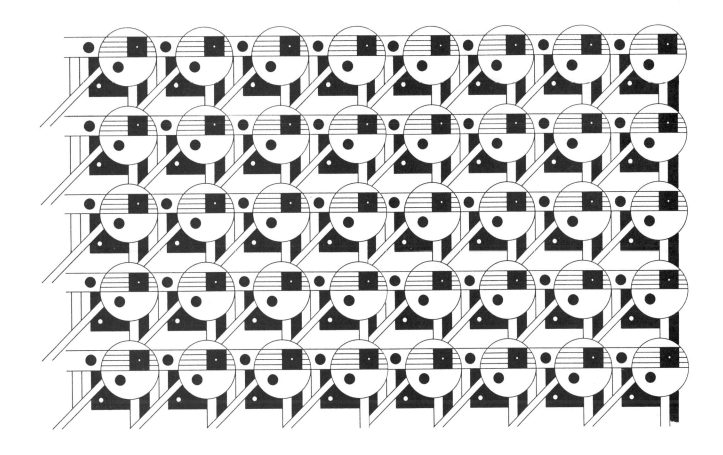

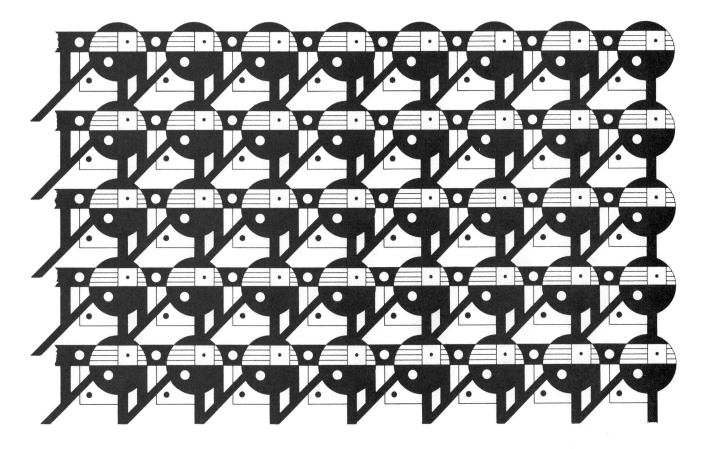

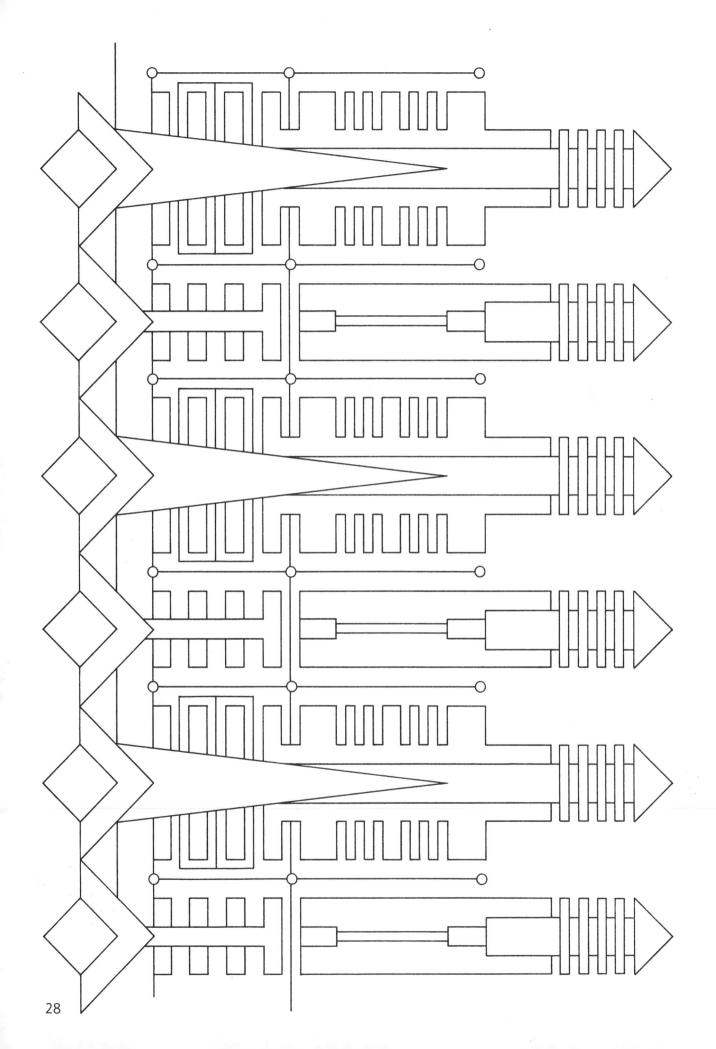

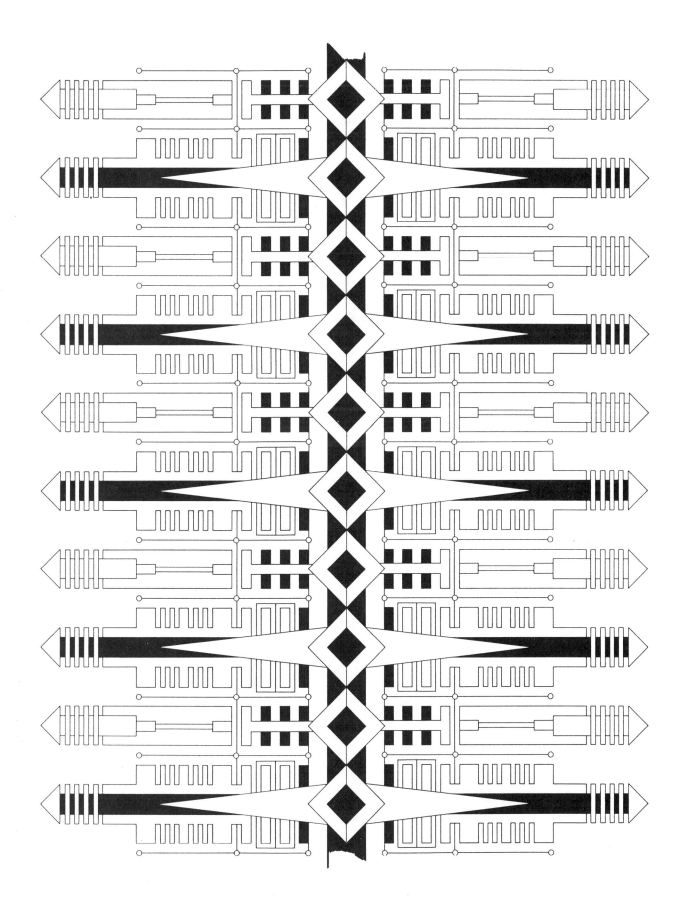

29

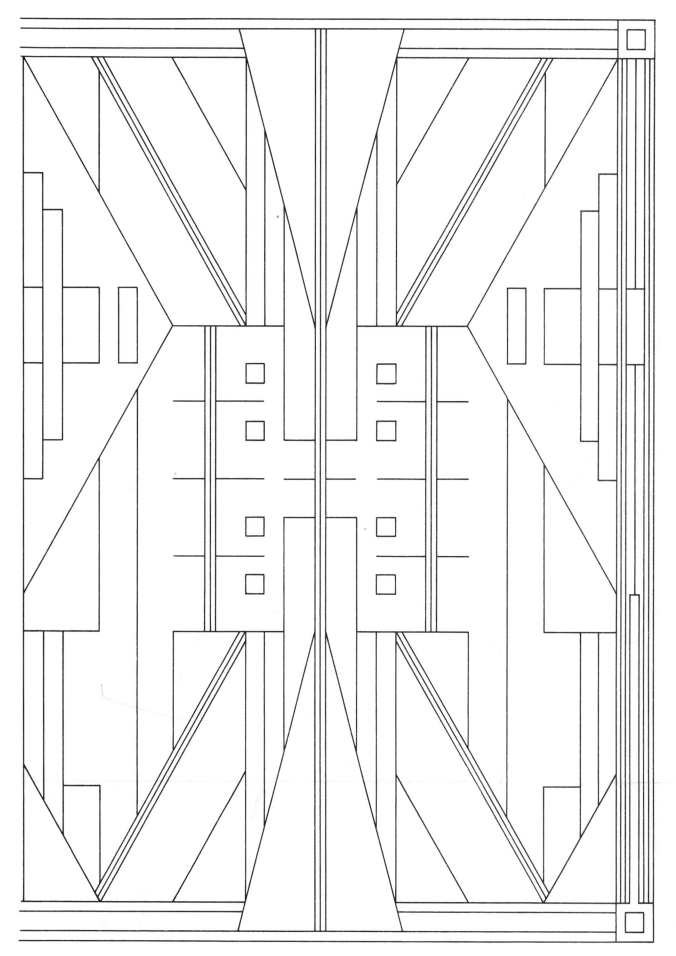

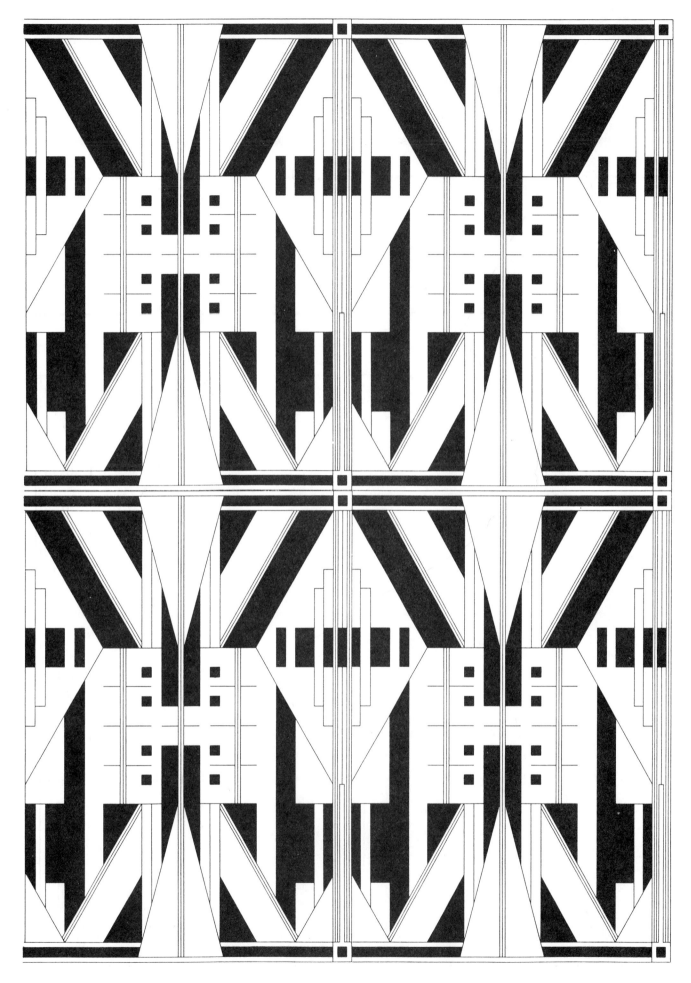

33

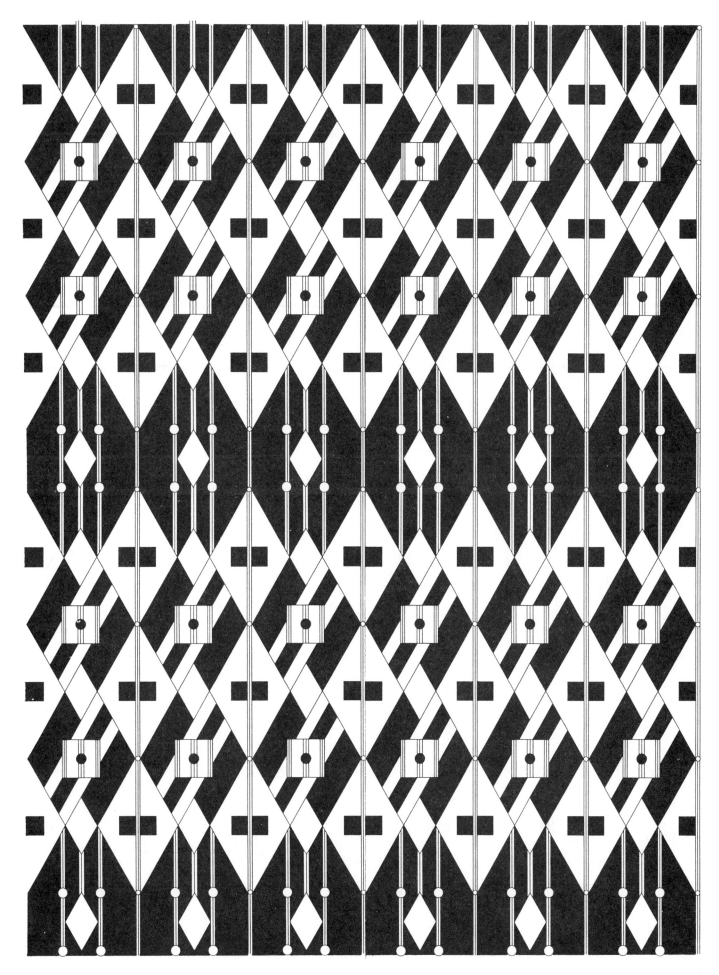

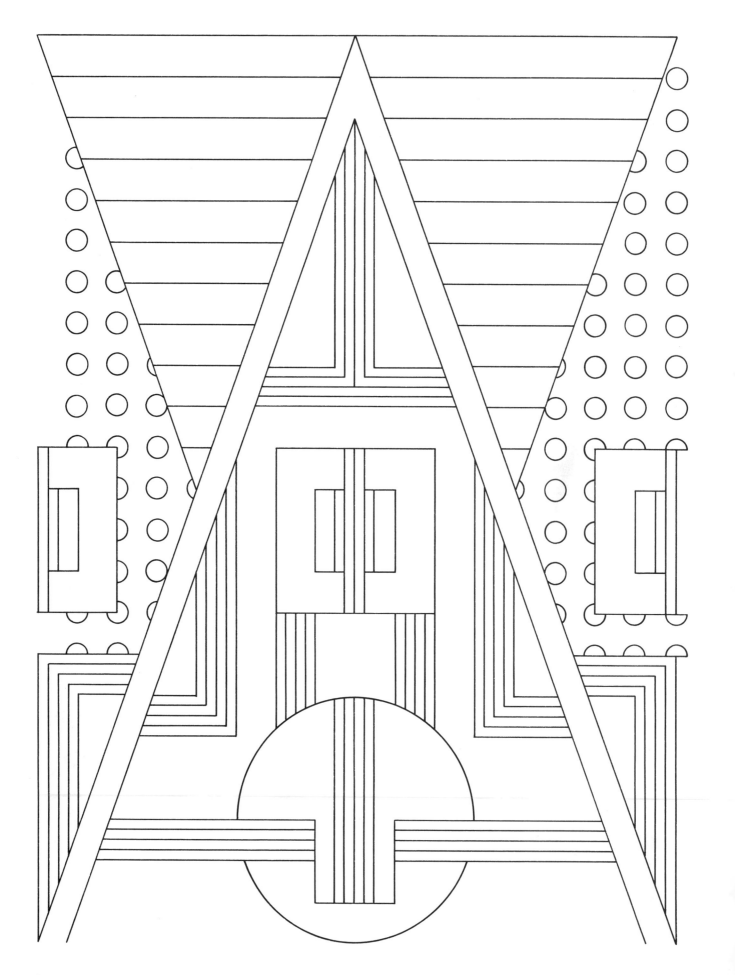

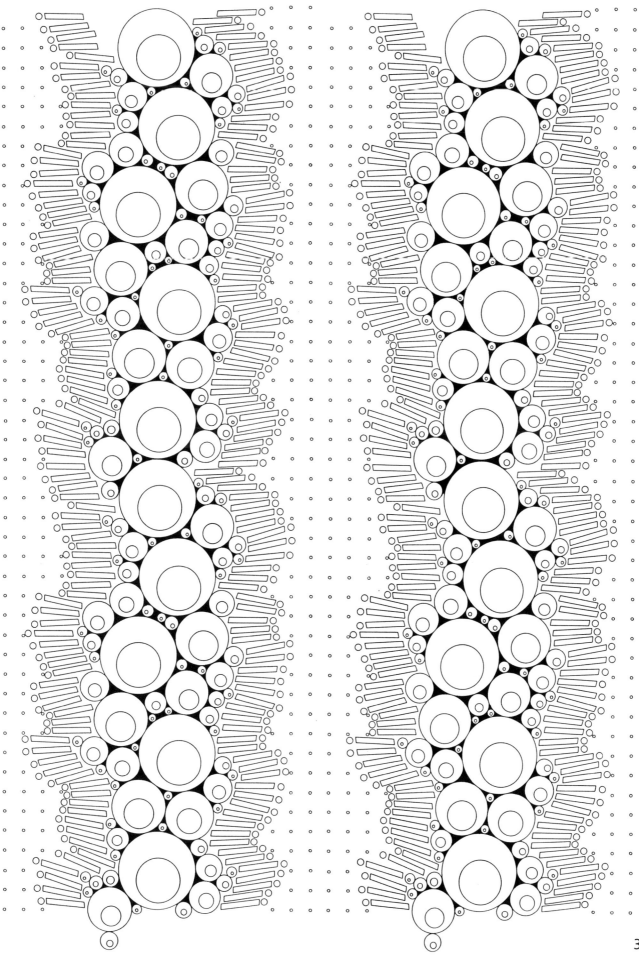

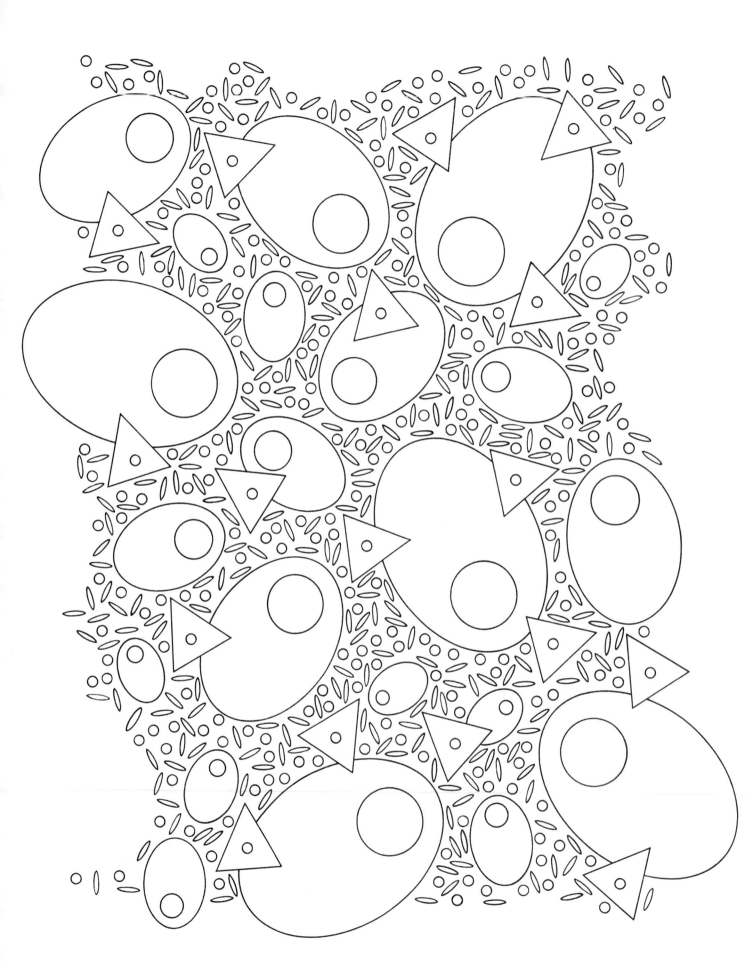

41

43

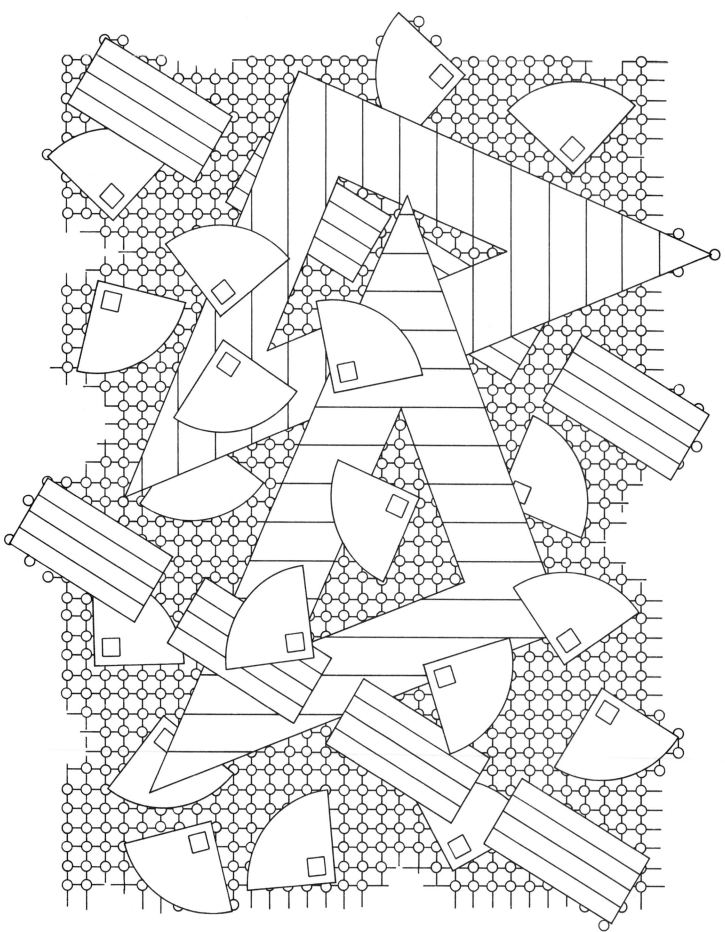

44